S.T.E.A.M.

THROUGH THE SEASONS

SPRING

ANNA CLAYBOURNE

WAYLAND
www.waylandbooks.co.uk

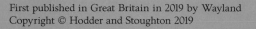

First published in Great Britain in 2019 by Wayland
Copyright © Hodder and Stoughton 2019

All rights reserved.

Senior Commissioning Editor: Melanie Palmer
Design: squareandcircus.co.uk
Illustrations: Supriya Sahai

HB ISBN 978 1 5263 0904 4
PB ISBN 978 1 5263 0905 1

Picture credits: Africa Studio/Shutterstock: 15b.
aluxum/istockphoto: 25t. Dekdoyjaidee/istockphoto: 13c.
Bartosz Hadyniak/istockphoto: 5c. Anton Jankovoy/
Shutterstock: 6b. kavalenkava /Shutterstock: 26b.
kudrashka-a/Shutterstock: 29c. leezsnow/istockphoto: 29b.
lovelyday12/Shutterstock: 9t. mediaphotos/istockphoto: 5t.
Rasical/istockphoto: 23t. shapecharge/istockphoto: 5b.
Thorsten Spoerlein/Shutterstock: 10b. stereohype/
istockphoto: 16b. Valentyn Volkov/Shutterstock: 19b.
Sean Xu/Shutterstock: 20b. Additional illustrations: Freepik

Every attempt has been made to clear copyright. Should
there be any inadvertent omission please apply to the
publisher for rectification.

MIX
Paper from
responsible sources
FSC® C104740
FSC
www.fsc.org

Printed in China

Wayland
An imprint of
Hachette Children's Group
Part of Hodder and Stoughton
Carmelite House
50 Victoria Embankment
London EC4Y 0DZ

An Hachette UK Company
www.hachette.co.uk

SAFETY INFORMATION:
Please ask an adult for help with
any activities that could be tricky,
involve cooking or handling
glass. Ask adult permission when
appropriate.

Due care has been taken to ensure
the activities are safe and the
publishers regret they cannot
accept liability for any loss or
injuries sustained.

Contents

SPRING!

In spring, the weather gets warmer and sunnier. The days are lighter for longer. There are rain showers too, helping to water the soil.

Nature in spring

As the ground warms up, plants start growing, and sprout new leaves and flowers.

Bees buzz around. Butterflies flutter, feeding on the flowers.

Birds sing to find a mate. They make nests, lay eggs, and baby chicks hatch out.

WHAT IS SPRING?

Like all the seasons, spring happens because of the way the Earth moves around the Sun.

The Earth orbits around the Sun once every year.

The Earth is tilted. As it moves around, different areas lean more towards the Sun.

When your part of the world starts leaning towards the Sun, it's spring where you live!

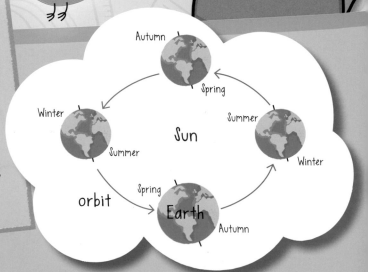

Autumn

Spring

Winter

Summer

Sun

Summer

Winter

orbit

Spring

Earth

Autumn

Spring festivals

Around the world, people celebrate the coming of spring with festivals and holidays. Easter, May Day, Holi, Nowruz and Hanami are all spring festivals.

Spring science

This book is full of fun science experiments, activities and things to make in spring.

You can do most of them with everyday craft materials and recycled objects from around the house. Turn to page 30 for some extra tips about materials and where to find them.

HAVE AN ADULT HANDY!

SOME OF THE ACTIVITIES INVOLVE SHARP OBJECTS, HEAT AND COOKING. MAKE SURE YOU ALWAYS HAVE AN ADULT TO HELP YOU, AND ASK THEM TO DO THESE PARTS.

MAKE A RAINBOW

In spring, you sometimes see a rainbow in the sky. Rainbows happen when sunlight shines through raindrops. Try making a mini rainbow at home, using a glass of water.

WHAT YOU NEED:

- A PLAIN GLASS
- A PIECE OF CARD, ABOUT THE SIZE OF A POSTCARD
- SCISSORS
- STICKY TAPE
- A JUG OF WATER
- A SUNNY WINDOW, WITH CURTAINS IF POSSIBLE
- A PIECE OF PLAIN WHITE PAPER

Step 1:

With an adult to help, cut a slot in the middle of the piece of card, like this. Tape the card to the glass so that the slot sticks up above the edge.

Spring science:
What is a rainbow?

Sunlight is made up of all the colours we can see, mixed together. When light shines in and out of water, it bends, or refracts. This makes it spread out and separate into a rainbow of colours.

Step 2:

Stand the glass by the window, with the card side towards the sunlight. If there are curtains, partly close them to make the room darker.

Step 3:

Using the jug, fill the glass to the top with water. Put the white paper in front of the glass.

Step 4:

Turn and move the glass until the sunlight shines through the slot on to the water surface. You should see rainbow colours on the paper.

What else can I make?

If you have a garden hose, you can make a rainbow outdoors on a sunny day. Switch the hose to the "mist" setting and stand with your back to the Sun. You should see a rainbow in the mist!

PLANTING SEEDS

Spring is the best time to plant seeds and see them grow. Here's an easy way to grow plants from seeds.

WHAT YOU NEED:
- GREEN OR RUNNER BEAN SEEDS FROM A SUPERMARKET OR GARDEN CENTRE
- A CLEAR GLASS JAR
- KITCHEN PAPER
- WATER
- A SUNNY WINDOW

Step 1:
Fold a piece of kitchen paper small enough to fit in the jar, and sprinkle water on it to make it damp. Put it around the inside of the jar, like this.

Step 2:
Push a bean seed down between the kitchen paper and the side of the jar. Sprinkle a bit more water on it.

Step 3:
Stand the jar in a sunny place, with the sunlight shining on the bean. Sprinkle more water on it every day ... and watch it grow!

Spring science: What makes seeds grow?

Seeds can last a long time without changing – in their packets, for example. But when a seed senses warmth, light and water, it will sprout, or germinate. Each seed contains a supply of food that helps the plant to start growing. Once it has leaves, they take in sunlight, and this gives the plant the energy it needs to get bigger and bigger.

What else can I make?

When your bean plant has several leaves, you can plant it into a larger pot, filled with compost. Make a hole in the compost for the roots, and gently push the compost back around them. The plant will grow in a sunny place indoors or outdoors.

HAIRY CATERPILLAR

This big, hairy caterpillar is made from grass. Make it outdoors if you can, as it's pretty messy!

WHAT YOU NEED:

- A BOX OF GRASS SEEDS
- A SMALL BAG OF POTTING COMPOST
- A LARGE SPOON
- SCISSORS
- AN OLD PAIR OF THIN TIGHTS
- ELASTIC BANDS
- PIPE CLEANERS AND GOOGLY EYES
- WATER IN A JUG OR WATERING CAN

Step 1:

Open the bag of compost, and add a big handful of grass seeds. Use the spoon to stir them in.

Spring science:
Hairy caterpillars

In spring, butterfly and moth caterpillars hatch from eggs and feed on plants. Some have long hairs to protect them from hunters. Some caterpillar hairs can sting – so never touch a hairy caterpillar!

Step 2:

Cut one leg off the tights. Ask an adult to hold the leg open, while you spoon the compost and seed mix into it.

Step 3:

When the leg is filled to about 30 cm, ask an adult to tie it tightly closed. Stretch elastic band around it to make body sections.

Step 4:

Put the caterpillar on the ground and soak it with water. Leave it in a sunny spot to grow, and water it every day.

Step 5:

As the grass grows, it will give your caterpillar long hair. Add pipe cleaner legs and googly eyes. If you like, give it a haircut too!

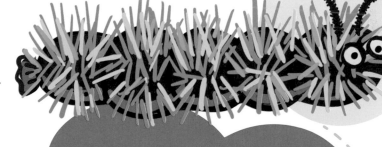

What else can I make?

Try making a hairy head. First, put grass seeds into the toe of a tights leg. Add enough compost to make a round ball and tie it closed. Sit it in a bowl and water it every day. When the hair grows, add a face!

FLOWER FLICK BOOK

In spring, lots of plants grow buds, which open out into colourful flowers. Flowers open slowly, but you can speed things up with a springtime flick book.

WHAT YOU NEED:

- A THICK PAD OF PLAIN STICKY NOTES, OR A SMALL BLANK NOTEPAD
- FELT-TIP PENS

Step 1:

First, look at some pictures of flowers opening out from buds, in books or on the Internet, to see how it works. Choose a flower to draw, or make up your own.

Step 2:

Turn to the last page of your pad, and draw a line of soil near the outer edge of the page. Draw a tiny plant starting to grow.

Step 3:

Turn to the page before. You should be able to just see your picture underneath. Draw another picture in the same place, but make the plant very slightly bigger.

Step 4:

Working back through the pages, draw the plant over and over again. Make the plant slowly grow bigger. Then, add a flower bud. Over many pages, make it open into a flower.

Step 5:

To see the flower opening, flick through the pad quickly from the back to the front. As the pictures whizz past, your brain puts them together, and it looks like a moving image.

Spring science:
What are flowers for?

Plants grow flowers to attract insects. As insects feed on nectar (a sweet liquid) inside flowers, they spread pollen, a yellow powder, between plants. This is called pollination, and it helps plants to make seeds.

What else can I make?
Try these flick book ideas:
- A chick hatching
- A tree growing
- A bee visiting a flower

SEE A LEAF BREATHE

As plants grow in the sunshine, their leaves actually breathe. They breathe in gases from the air, and breathe out other gases and water. You can't see it by looking, but you can with this experiment.

WHAT YOU NEED:

- A LARGE PLASTIC FOOD STORAGE BAG
- STICKY TAPE
- A TREE OR LARGE PLANT WITH LEAVES YOU CAN REACH

Step 1:

Hold a branch of the tree or plant still, and put the bag over the end, so that there are several leaves inside.

Step 2:

Use sticky tape to hold the bag closed and make sure it stays on the tree.

Step 3:

If it's nice and sunny, leave the bag there all day. If it's not very sunny, leave it for two or three days.

Step 4:

Check inside the bag. It should contain water. The leaves have breathed out water vapour (a gas), which collects on the sides of the bag as a liquid.

Photosynthesis

Leaf takes in:

Energy from sunlight

Carbon dioxide gas

Water from the soil

Leaf gives out:

Food for plant

Oxygen gas

Water vapour (gas)

Stomata

Spring science:
In and out

Plants live and grow using energy from the sun. This is called photosynthesis. To do it, they also use other chemicals, which go in and out of the plant's leaves. Gases leave and enter the leaf through tiny holes, called stomata.

What else can I make?

If you put a leaf in a glass of water and stand it in the sunshine, you'll see bubbles of gas forming on the leaf's surface. This is oxygen being breathed out.

INK AND WATER FLOWERS

Spring flowers have bright colours to help bees and other insects find them. Make these pretty paper flowers with a bit of simple colour science ...

WHAT YOU NEED:
- PAPER COFFEE FILTERS (THE KIND THAT OPEN OUT FLAT) OR KITCHEN PAPER
- WATER-WASHABLE FELT-TIP PENS
- WATER
- A SMALL DISH OR BOWL
- SCISSORS
- STRING
- PIPE CLEANERS

Step 1:
If you're using coffee filters, open them out flat. If you're using kitchen paper, cut circles out of it, about 10 cm across.

Step 2:
In the middle of each circle, use felt-tip pens to draw a dot, a circle or a simple flower shape, like these.

Spring science: Ink and water

Most ink is made up of different chemicals and colours. Some of these chemicals spread out through the paper more than others, so you see a range of different colours. Black and dark felt-tip pens work best!

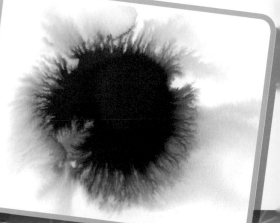

Step 3:

Put some water in the bottom of your dish, and lie the paper on top. Gently push down the middle, where the pen marks are, so that it touches the water.

Step 4:

Leave the paper for several minutes. The water will spread out through it, making the ink spread out, too.

Step 5:

When you've done this with all your circles, leave them to dry. Then you can cut them into flower shapes, like these.

What else can I make?

You can add pipe cleaner stalks to your flower. Or make butterflies by wrapping pipe cleaners around the middle of a paper circle, using the ends as the antennae.

RAIN IN A JAR

In spring the weather gets warmer and sunnier, but it can be rainy too. This experiment shows how rain works, and where it comes from.

WHAT YOU NEED:

- A CLEAR GLASS JAR OR TUMBLER
- THE LID FOR THE JAR, OR A SAUCER
- WARM TAP WATER
- ICE CUBES

Step 1:

Fill the jar about 1/4 full with water from the hot tap. Stand it in a safe place.

Spring science:
the water cycle

The jar is a tiny version of the world. Some of the water in seas and rivers escapes into the air as a gas, called water vapour – especially when it's warmed by the sun. The gas rises into the sky, where it cools down, and forms clouds. As they get colder, the water turns back into drops of liquid, and they fall as rain.

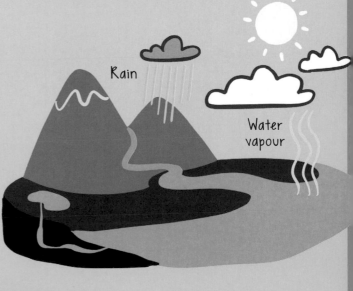

Rain

Water vapour

Step 2:

Put the lid on top, turned the wrong way up. If you don't have a lid, use a saucer.

Step 3:

Make sure the lid or saucer covers the edges of the jar, with no gaps. After a few minutes, the inside of the jar will start to look cloudy.

Step 4:

Carefully put a few ice cubes on top of the lid or saucer – as many as you can fit on to it. After a while, raindrops will form and drop back down, or run down the sides.

What else can I make?

Try the same experiment with cold water. Does it take longer to make rain?

BALANCING BUTTERFLY

Butterflies land on flowers to suck nectar from them, using their long, straw-like tongues. This butterfly will balance on your fingertip, or on the end of a pencil.

WHAT YOU NEED:

- THICK CARD (PURPLE OR WHITE)
- TRACING PAPER OR GREASEPROOF PAPER
- A PENCIL
- SCISSORS
- COLOURING PENS OR PENCILS
- TWO SMALL COINS
- STICKY TAPE OR STRONG GLUE

Step 1:

Use tracing paper or greaseproof paper to trace this butterfly shape. Carefully cut out your butterfly shape, and draw around it on to thick card.

Spring science: Balancing wings

When the butterfly balances, it looks impossible! But things will balance as long as their weight is spread evenly around the balancing point. The coins make the wingtips as heavy as the rest of the butterfly, so its balancing point is on its head.

Step 2:

Cut out your card butterfly too. If it's hard to cut, ask an adult to help. Colour the butterfly in with bright colours and patterns.

Step 3:

Use Sticky tape or glue to fix two coins underneath the butterfly's wingtips, in the places shown by the two dots.

Step 4:

You can now balance the butterfly by putting its head on the tip of your finger, like this. It will also work on the blunt or eraser end of a pencil.

What else can I make?

Using the same method, can you make a balancing ...

- Dragonfly
- Bird
- Bat?

TORNADO IN A BOTTLE

A tornado is a powerful windstorm that swirls around in a spiral. They can happen anywhere, at any time – but they are most common in North America in late spring. It's easy to make your own mini tornado inside a bottle (and much safer!).

WHAT YOU NEED:

- TWO MATCHING PLASTIC DRINKS BOTTLES
- WATER
- STRONG PACKING TAPE OR DUCT TAPE
- A SMALL PACK OF GLITTER (OPTIONAL)

Step 1:

Fill one of the bottles 3/4 full with water. Pour the glitter into the bottle as well, if you're using it.

Step 2:

Turn the other bottle upside-down and stand it on top of the first one, so that the openings line up exactly.

Spring science:
Spiral power

Tornadoes happen when warm and cool air meet, and start to spiral around each other. The more they spiral, the faster the winds go.

In the bottle, the swirling movement makes the water spiral around like a tornado. The glitter makes it easier to see.

Step 4:

Hold both bottles, turn them upside down, and swirl the top bottle round and round to make the water inside spin. You should see a tornado!

What else can I make?

Tornado winds can be so strong, they pick up people and even cars. Try adding tiny plasticine people or cars to your tornado in a bottle.

Step 3:

With an adult to help, use plenty of strong tape to fix the two bottles together tightly, so that water can't leak out.

EGG DECORATING

There are several spring festivals around the world, including Holi, Easter and Nowruz ... and these festivals often involve eggs. They are a symbol of spring and new birth, as spring is when many types of bird lay their eggs.

WHAT YOU NEED:

- EGGS (WHITE OR PALE IN COLOUR IF POSSIBLE)
- A SAUCEPAN
- A COOKER
- A BOWL OF WATER
- AN ADULT TO BOIL THE EGGS
- A TEA TOWEL
- FELT-TIP OR MARKER PENS

Step 2:

Cool the eggs by leaving them in a bowl of cold water for another 10 minutes.

Step 1:

Ask an adult to boil the eggs in a pan of water for about 10 minutes. This will make them hard-boiled and solid all the way through.

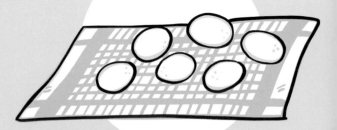

Step 3:

Dry them well on a tea towel.

Spring science:
Eggs and babies

It's not just birds that lay eggs – other animals do too, including crocodiles, turtles, frogs and many types of fish, insect and spider. So did dinosaurs! Eggs have a shell or covering that keeps the baby inside safe as it grows. They also contain a supply of food for it to eat.

Step 4:

Use felt-tip or marker pens to decorate your eggs with colours and patterns. The eggs below might give you some ideas!

What else can I do?

You can save your decorated eggs, or use them for an egg race! Take your eggs to the top of a grassy slope in a park, garden or playground. On the count of three, everyone rolls their eggs down the slope. Whose goes furthest?

EGG STRENGTH TEST

Eggs are famous for being delicate and easy to break, but they are actually quite strong! You might be surprised by how much weight an eggshell can hold.

WHAT YOU NEED:

- 4 EGGS
- OLD TOWELS OR TEA TOWELS
- A LARGE HARDBACK BOOK
- LOTS MORE BOOKS

Step 1:

Ask an adult to break the eggs in half as neatly as possible, and wash the eggshell halves in soap and water. (Save the insides of the eggs for cooking.)

Spring science:
Eggstra strong!

An eggshell will break if you hit the side of it, but if you press down on top of it, it's very strong. An egg's shape makes pressure spread all around it, so it can hold a heavy weight.

Architects have copied the strong shape of an egg to make dome-shaped roofs, like this.

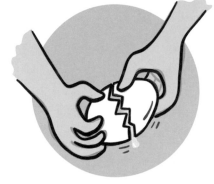

Step 2:

Take the rounded, less pointy eggshell halves, and break off any sticking-out pieces of shell, to make them as neat as possible.

Step 3:

Spread out a few old towels or tea towels on the floor to make a soft surface. Stand your four eggshell halves on top.

Step 4:

Rest your large hardback book on top of the eggshells, with one at each corner. How many more books do you think you could pile on top of it before the eggshells break?

Step 5:

Add more books on top of the first one, one by one. Count how many the eggshells will support without breaking.

What else can I do?

If you think your eggs are strong enough, you could try standing on the books.

MAKE A KALEIDOSCOPE

Catch the sunlight in a kaleidoscope to see swirling reflected patterns.

WHAT YOU NEED:

- A CARDBOARD KITCHEN ROLL TUBE
- A SHEET OF SILVER OR GOLD CARD
- A PENCIL
- A RULER
- SCISSORS
- STICKY TAPE
- A MARKER PEN
- BLACK CARD
- A DISPOSABLE PLASTIC BOTTLE
- SEQUINS, GLITTER, SWEET WRAPPERS
- TRACING OR GREASEPROOF PAPER

Step 1:

Measure the width of the cardboard tube. On one end of the shiny card, mark four equal sections, slightly narrower than the width of the tube, like this.

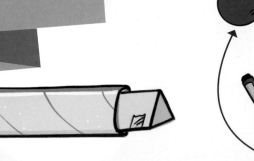

Step 2:

Cut off the rest of the card, and fold along the lines to make a prism with the shiny side inside. Tape it together, and push it into the cardboard tube.

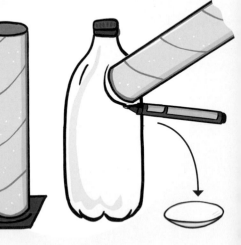

Step 3:

Draw around the end of the tube on to black card. Repeat to draw a circle on the smooth, curved part of the plastic bottle. Cut these circles out (ask an adult to help with cutting the bottle).

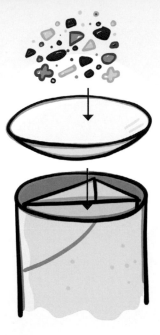

Step 4:

Put the plastic circle on one end of the tube, with the curved side facing in, like a dish. Put some sequins, glitter and cut-up sweet wrappers into it.

Step 5:

Cut a larger circle of tracing or greaseproof paper, and wrap it over the end, trapping the sequins, glitter and warppers inside. Use sticky tape to fix it to the tube.

Step 6:

Use a sharp pencil to make a small hole in the middle of the black card circle. Fix it over the other end of the tube using sticky tape.

To use the kaleidoscope, point it at the sky or a bright lamp, look through the hole, and turn the tube around. But never look directly at the sun!

Spring science:
Reflecting light

When light hits shiny surfaces, it bounces, or reflects, off them. The patterns in the kaleidoscope are made by light from the moving objects reflecting off the silver card as you turn the tube around.

MATERIALS

This list gives you ideas about where to look for the materials you need for the activities in this book.

BASIC ART AND CRAFT MATERIALS:

- PAPER
- FELT-TIP PENS
- MARKER PENS
- COLOURED PENCILS
- SCISSORS
- GLUE
- STICKY TAPE

FROM A CRAFT OR HOBBY SHOP:

- BLACK, WHITE AND COLOURED CARD
- SILVER CARD
- SEQUINS, GLITTER, SHINY BEADS
- TRACING PAPER
- PIPE CLEANERS
- GOOGLY EYES

FROM THE KITCHEN:

- GLASSES, BOWLS, JUGS,
- PLATES AND SAUCERS
- TRAY
- WATER
- ICE CUBES
- PLASTIC BOTTLES
- KITCHEN ROLL (KITCHEN PAPER)
- GREASEPROOF PAPER
- FOOD STORAGE BAGS
- EGGS
- TEA TOWELS
- SAUCEPAN
- COOKER

FROM AROUND THE HOUSE:

- COINS
- PACKING TAPE OR DUCT TAPE
- SWEET WRAPPERS
- STICKY NOTES
- BOOKS
- ELASTIC BANDS
- OLD TIGHTS

FROM A SUPERMARKET OR GARDEN CENTRE:

- SEEDS
- POTTING COMPOST

Glossary

architect Someone who designs buildings.

balancing point The part of an object that it can balance on.

bud Part of a plant that opens out into a flower.

carbon dioxide A type of gas that is found in the air, and used by plants.

compost Dead leaves, plant parts or food that have decayed and turned into rich soil.

germinate To start growing. A seed germinates when it starts to grow and put out shoots and roots.

hatch To break out of an egg.

nectar A sweet liquid made inside flowers to attract insects and other animals.

orbit To circle around another object, such as a planet orbiting around the sun.

oxygen A type of gas that is found in the air, and released by plants.

photosynthesis The way plants make their own food using water, gases from the air, and sunlight.

pollen A yellow powder made by flowers, and used in making seeds.

pollination Moving pollen from one flower to another, which helps plants to make seeds.

reflect To bounce off a surface. Light reflects off mirrors and other surfaces.

refract To bend. Light refracts as it passes from one clear substance (such as air glass, or water) into another.

stomata Tiny holes in leaves, which let gases in and out.

tornado A powerful windstorm in the shape of a swirling spiral.

water vapour Water in the form of a gas. Water vapour is found in the air and released by plants.

Index